Michael Winicott

HENRY FORD: ENTERPRENEURSHIP LESSONS

Teachings from one of the most successful entrepreneurs in the world

© 2015 by Michael Winicott.

Published by UNITEXTO

UNITEXTO
Digital Publishing

TABLE OF CONTENTS

Introduction

Henry Ford-The Great Entrepreneur
A Summary of the Man
The Greatest Invention
The Secrets Revealed
The Beginning of Your Journey

Lesson #1: Make the Leap!

December 1879
Risk is Necessary for Success
Make the Move
The Tipping Point of Success
Chapter Summary

Lesson #2: People are Assets

April 1888
Only the Right People
Make it a Win-Win
People Create Purpose
Chapter Summary:

Lesson #3: Fight, Fight, Fight!

June 1896
It Takes More than Just a Great Work Ethic
Rejoice in Failure
Chapter Summary:

Lesson #4: Proximity is Destiny

October 1901

Perfection is Useless While Hidden

Trust Yourself

Chapter Summary:

Lesson #5: Never let go of the Dream

1903-1908

Never Stop Your Momentum

Investigate Every Opportunity

Chapter Summary:

Lesson #6: Share the Wealth

January 1914

Share the Knowledge

Chapter Summary:

Lesson #7: Learn how to fail

November 1915

Entrepreneurs Don't Give Up

Every Failure Brings Future Success

Chapter Summary:

Lesson #8: Be Quick or be Dead

March 1919

Insight Creates Opportunities

Be Prepared for Others to Fail

Chapter Summary:

Lesson #9: Don't get Caught Up!

March 1927

Be an Entrepreneur for Others

Don't Let Your Momentum Fall

Chapter Summary:

Lesson #10: It's More than Money

October 1929
It's Not Always About Money
Some Dreams Don't Require a Business
Chapter Summary:

Conclution: The Power is Yours

The Legacy of Henry Ford
Create Your Legacy
The Final Words

Introduction

Thanks for taking the time to be here with us. In the next pages, you will take a journey that will show you the most important facts of the life of the genius Henry Ford. You will also see the best lessons we can extract from his unique experience.

Why do we write about Henry Ford?

Simply because this kind of leaders serve as great inspiration for others. We trust that this book will impact your life in the best way possible. Every dream is possible, and we believe that the best way to start a path to fulfilling yours is by learning what the great men in history have done.

Welcome to this amazing story!

Henry Ford-The Great Entrepreneur

A Summary of the Man

Henry Ford was an inventor known by the entire world. He created one of the most popular automobiles of the early 20th century, the Model T, and designed the beginnings of what is now the assembly line used in today's factories.

Ford is one of the best examples of someone who created something out of nothing. He had little to no education, and held nothing but a passion for machinery at a young age, which he pursued throughout his entire lifetime. He spent more hours of labor on his inventions in two years than most people spend in a life time. His dedication to his art made his dreams blossom, and from the beginning of the founding of Ford Motor Company to its end, Henry Ford was always improving, and always creating.

Ford grew up in Michigan, a state that has grown into the largest automobile manufacturing economy in the United States. His passion for machinery brought him to Detroit, the heart of the automobile industry, where he studied and learned about manufacturing as an apprentice machinist.

Through this experience, he learned about the "how" and the "why" of the steam engine, and from there set off on his own personal journey to discover a way to build a horseless carriage.

The Greatest Invention

The technology and innovation that went into the early 20th century car production expanded beyond its industry, and the methods used by Henry Ford's automobile factories became the standard procedure for every factory in the United States for decades. The assembly line was one of the most powerful inventions in the early 20th century, and it sparked the epitome of the industrial revolution that would help better prepare the United States for the World Wars.

Henry Ford was beyond just an entrepreneur: he was an inventor, a leader, and a man of respect both inside and outside of his industry. His accomplishments originated from the knowledge that he had of himself, and the courage to take the risk to become something bigger. Henry Ford is an inspiration to the world, and his legacy continues to live on through Ford Motor Company.

The Secrets Revealed

It took more than just a few great decisions to become the great man that Henry Ford was. The combination of obstacles and decisions refined him, and turned him into a machine for success. The moments in his life that are the most inspirational are the moments that most defined him as an entrepreneur. Through his lens, we can unveil the secrets that built him into the strong businessman that created Ford Motor Company.

This book will unlock the secrets of becoming an entrepreneur, through the experiences of Henry Ford's life. These experiences show the necessary components that are required for an entrepreneur to thrive and succeed in a world of business and growth. As the story of Henry Ford unfolds, so too will the knowledge to go forth and succeed as an innovator.

Each chapter will reveal a piece of the puzzle that will unlock the elements needed to be successful in your ventures. This will be a journey of discovery about how to think as an entrepreneur, and what it takes to use your mind to get there. Henry Ford will be used as a reflection of the choices and decisions that you need to make to exceed beyond that of the average person, and become truly great.

The Beginning of Your Journey

Before you begin delving into this book. It is important that you have a goal in mind to mold and develop as we venture on through the chapters. Henry Ford led an inspiring life, and provided a lifetime of knowledge and experiences that can aid you in the fight for success as an entrepreneur. But it can only work effectively if you have that purpose in mind.

Finding a strong, unmovable goal at the beginning of this book will maximize the amount of knowledge and power that you take from the life of Henry Ford.Just as Henry Ford left his family to pursue his passion for machines, you too will soon be seeking your goal that is hidden in the opportunities we find in this world. This gold will be revealed through the eyes of Henry Ford.

Lesson #1: Make the Leap!

December 1879

It was the deciding moment of Henry Ford's life. He had been raised in the dull environment of the farming culture, unable to pursue his dreams. His infatuation for machinery was limited in this setting, and Ford decided that the only way to pursue his dreams was to leave his home and set off on his own.

With this in mind, at the end of the year Henry Ford left his farm home, and set off for Detroit, where the booming industry of machinery was accelerating. At the age of 16, Ford took off and left the world of farming behind him, in search for new opportunities elsewhere.

Ford arrived in Detroit, and took on an apprenticeship with a machinist. His natural talent for the art grew, and he quickly became a part of the machine industry, grabbing a job at Edison Illuminating Company, and becoming chief engineer in 1893. There he began his plans to create his idea of the horseless carriage. It all became possible because of his decision to leave the comfort of his farming home and seek riches elsewhere.

Think of the life that Henry Ford would have lived, had he not made the decision to reach beyond his comfort zone and explore? Ford knew that machinery was something that he wanted to pursue, and he made the decision that he wanted to dedicate his life to the industry. However, he never would have gotten the opportunity to accomplish the feats that he did, until he made the decision to take the leap of faith into a new, unknown world.

Like Ford, many entrepreneurs have their passion figured out, and they know exactly what they want to pursue in life to accomplish their dreams, but they are simply just not in the right environment for what they want to pursue. It would have been impossible for Ford to have made an impact on the automobile industry in the small, rural life of his farm.

Risk is Necessary for Success

To be successful, we learn from Ford that you must take that risk. This means that you must be willing to make the jump in any direction without hesitation. Ford moved himself from the small quiet farm to the bustling urban city of Detroit! Could you imagine the fear that must have been in his mind?

That fear that he felt, is a fear that all entrepreneurs feel. It is the questionable doubt that keeps us back and slows us down. It is the chiming in our head to do what is safe, and what is the most comfortable. As charming as this voice in our head may seem, it is absolutely necessary that we do not listen to that voice. We must reach out beyond our comfort zone to gain the riches that we desire.

Make the Move

Being open-minded as an entrepreneur is necessary to allow yourself to see these opportunities for escape. Ford could have chosen to stay at the farm and pursue machinery on his own just as easily as you could choose to pursue your dreams in your hometown instead of elsewhere. The easiest option always seems to be the better option to the one who wants to "Get rich quick". However, as an entrepreneur, you must understand that pursuing goals requires difficulty, and desperation to complete them.

Think of an area that would be more prosperous for your dreams, and be open-minded to the possibility of living there. A change in environment can drastically accelerate your productivity, and it can bring you to new opportunities that you have never before seen.

The Tipping Point of Success

When we discuss risk in this chapter, we are using Ford's decision to move to another location as an example. But the element of risk goes further than the decision to relocate. It goes into many elements of an entrepreneur's life. When it comes to making an enormous impact on the world with your inventions or products, risk plays the most important role.

The tipping point is used in a lot of books to describe why success is so necessary. Ford had lived his entire childhood filled with a passion for machinery, and grew in him the desire to do more with his life, and make an impact in the world using his passion. A "now or never" moment came to him, and it was then and there that he needed to make the jump or fall back.

The key point as an entrepreneur is to take a planned risk. When you play with slot machines, you are taking an unplanned risk, and one that you will more often than not lose with each attempt. Fortunately for you, entrepreneurial adventures isn't a game that is uncontrollable. Everything that you do is controllable, and almost every element can be taken into account to increase your chances of success, and bring your ideas to a tipping point.

Chapter Summary

- **Risk is necessary for success**
- **Do not be afraid to take risks**
- **Being Open-minded brings more opportunities**

- The larger the impact, the larger the risk
- Risks without plans are risky
- Planned risks increases the chance for success

Lesson #2: People are Assets

April 1888

After making the decision to move to Detroit, Henry Ford joined in the machine industry and began his journey as an apprentice. He refined his skill, and prepared himself for his future in the automobile industry. His life changed drastically within a short few years as he met a woman by the name of Clara Bryant, and eventually married in her 1888. Although Henry Ford was strong minded in his will to achieve success, he realized that the stressful environment of entrepreneurship required a rock on which he could stand, and could retreat to during his journey.

Henry Ford continued his apprenticeship, until his first child, Edsel, came into his life. With the need to support his family, Ford temporarily retreated back to his farm. He did this willingly, because his family became the pinnacle for his dreams. He lived at his ranch until he was hired on at Edison Illuminating Company, where he quickly moved up the ranks.

Whether it is a friend, a colleague, a family member, or a significant other, entrepreneurs need the support of another mind to help in their progress. Having an addition makes an exponential difference in your productivity, and helps produce more creative ideas than you would be able to do on your own.

The power of putting more than one mind together is infinite, and each member you add to your thinking machine, the more powerful your ideas will become. Taking different perspectives of multiple people and adding it into an equation will produce valuable results. Find the right person to interact in harmonious productivity, and you could be looking at a very bright future ahead of you.

Only the Right People

When you choose colleagues to work with, make sure that these people are beneficial. All too often people surround themselves with negative influences, that are nothing but detrimental to their passions. Be very meticulous when deciding who to keep in your life.

Look for fire, and you will get fire. However, if you're trying to keep your fire lit, and you jump in the ocean, there will be nothing left. This means that when you choose people to become assets, make sure that they share the same fire as you do. Their passions should be similar or harmonious to yours, and they should have the same level of support as you have for your dreams. Ford's wife would not have been with Ford, had she not had the support for Ford's great dreams.

Make it a Win-Win

An entrepreneur is meant to create value, and by doing so, they too get rewarded for their success. This is a very important moral standard that should guide your life as an entrepreneur. Everyone you meet, and every person that becomes part of your system should be rewarded.

Extortion and taking advantage of other people and companies is very prominent in the business world. As unethical as it is, it populates every industry, and hurts many people's dreams as they are innocently brought into a win-lose situation. As a true entrepreneur, you should always look to solve problems in a way that leaves everyone with a win-win situation. The perfect solution to a problem will always be the one that brings about the most benefits to everyone involved.

Every decision you make should be considerate to your colleagues, and those that surround you. Find ways to involve your supporters in your work, and share the rewards when you receive them. We will touch more on this in detail in a later chapter.

People Create Purpose

Ford left his farming family because of his distaste for that kind of labor. He left for Detroit because he wanted to pursue machinery and better his life. However, once his marriage brought about a child that needed to be taken care of, he went back to the life that he despised. He made this choice because he held his family in his mind as the fuel for his growing fire.

Using people you care about as an instigator to create movement is one of the most powerful ways to spark inspiration in the mind of an entrepreneur. Whether it be through affection or through friendship, putting other people at the forefront for your reasoning behind your actions will motivate you constantly. Ford made that difficult decision because he loved his wife and his child, and he continued to use them as he pushed on to become successful. He used their entity as the driving force behind his will to succeed.

Love is the strongest incentive to succeed. Ford's decision to marry Clara was because he loved her, but beyond just the affection, Ford's marriage with Clara was a strategic one for an entrepreneur. It gave him a purpose to create the things that he went on to create. Love is a driving force that can bring new ideas and feelings inside of you that otherwise would not come to be.

Chapter Summary:

- People are assets
- People will bring more ideas
- People will bring more productivity
- People will bring more opportunities
- Find people that are equally as passionate
- Make your endeavors a win-win for everyone
- Find someone that can support and be accountable for you
- Love is the strongest motivation for movement

Lesson #3: Fight, Fight, Fight!

June 1896

With an array of free time from his new promotion to chief engineer, Ford began churning his mind towards his dream at an exceptionally inspiring pace. He research regarding gasoline engines would prove key in realizing his dreams.

After two years of nonstop work, Ford had created his first ever version of a "horseless carriage". He named it the Ford Quadricycle, and took it to Edison investors. This visit generated such interest that he met Thomas Edison himself. Edison admired Ford's work, but encouraged him to continue improving the quadricycle into something even more superb. Ford complied with Edison's request, and over the following 2 years, created an even better automobile than the quadricycle.

With this second iteration, and after four years of never-ending labor and improving upon his ideas, Ford finally came to realize his dream. With this second vehicle, he would go on to eventually create the Ford Motor Company, and produce the astounding feats that are marked down in the history books. None of this would have been done without his tireless inspiration.

This is one of the simplest lessons to teach an entrepreneur. Most would read this, scoff at how unnecessary it is, and then move on to the next chapter. But little do these entrepreneurs know how important it is to continue digesting this concept in their minds. Without this foundation, entrepreneurs do not exist, and a dark world it would be without the accomplishments of entrepreneurs.

Henry Ford demonstrated rare degree of determination. For years, Ford worked, failed, improved, and failed again. He dedicated four years of his life to an idea that most others around him did not believe in.

It Takes More than Just a Great Work Ethic

If you think that you can take on a dream of yours with just a solid work ethic, then prepare to fail just as many times as Henry Ford did. No one can escape the inevitable obstacle of failure. But for the grand majority, failure becomes the end of their journey. They pack their things at the first sight of trouble, and leave their projects in the dust, seeing it as a broken dream that will never come to be.

Entrepreneurs that wish to succeed must hold much more within themselves then a solid work ethic. It takes an undying passion that will continuously fuel the fire of your inspiration, and revive your motivation daily. Henry Ford brought his first automobile to the greatest inventor of all time with the idea that he had fulfilled his dreams. When Edison proposed a better one, Ford simply continued pressing forward.

For most of you, that disheartening news that your first draft isn't there yet would crush that fiery motivation. Ford, however, simply grabbed his automobile and made it better. This is the attitude that an entrepreneur needs to succeed at what he does. Never stop improving your idea, and never stop creating a better version of you and your dreams.

This passion that drives you forward will serve to better your productivity, better your opportunities, and better your life as you search and find new and brighter ideas to pursue. It will amaze you how little you care about failure when you find an idea that truly means something to you. Being an entrepreneur without passion is similar to driving an automobile without gas: you will be going nowhere, because there is no fuel to make it move.

Rejoice in Failure

The fundamental lesson that can be found in this chapter is the acceptance of failure, which we will touch more on in a later chapter. There will rarely be a time that an entrepreneur embarks on a journey and does not experience some form of failure. The world only allows the brightest minds with the strongest wills to make their way to the top to claim their dreams. Because of this, entrepreneurs must not only be comfortable with failure, they must rejoice in it.

While the average person would see failure as the point at which to stop, entrepreneurs see failure as a point to continue going, and to continue with even more passion and direction. Failure is not an end, and this statement must always be in your mind as you confront obstacles. Failure is life's test to filter out the wannabe's from the true hardened dreamers that stick with their passions and knock down anything in their way to achieve success.

Put failure into perspective as a component of the entrepreneurship equation. Failure is a sign of improvement, and a milestone to represent the fact that you have momentum in your dream. When you fail, it should be seen as another opportunity to improve upon your idea until it reaches its maximum potential. The final product is what entrepreneurs look at. Viewing your goals in the perspective of the long-term future instead of the short-term "get rich quick" aspect will help make failure seem more like an obstacle to conquer instead of a game changing blow.

Chapter Summary:

- **Entrepreneurs must be willing to fight for their dream**
- **Nothing can be accomplished without determination**
- **It takes more than work ethic to succeed**
- **Passion and persistence are key factors to success**
- **Your passion should bring inspiration daily**
- **Ideas should always be improved**
- **Failure does not mean the end**
- **Failure is a filter between wannabe's and winners**
- **Use failure to your advantage**

Lesson #4: Proximity is Destiny

October 1901

Once the idea had finally materialized, Henry Ford exploded with progress on his horseless carriage. He persisted through his first model and finally came upon a second model, which proved to be much more efficient. With his hard earned work came the growing attention from the players of the automobile industry.

Ford created a 26 horsepower carriage that was entered into a race at Grosse point. It was a 10 mile race of other automobile inventors like Ford. His victory in the race brought even more attention to his inventions, and his publicity began to take him to much greater heights.

With the momentum that had come from his victory at Grosse Pointe, Ford created an even greater automobile, the 999. In 1902, it broke the American speed record. The 5 mile course was completed in five minutes and twenty eight seconds. This incredible accomplishment catapulted Henry Ford as a celebrity among the automobile industry. After many years of hard work, his inventions had finally made big news. This publicity would lead Ford to networking with industry players and investors and would ultimately lead to the incorporation of the Ford Motor Company.

Ford had created his first horseless carriage in 1896, and in 7 years he advanced from a first time inventor to a company owner that was on par with the rest of the industry.

But how did Ford reach that tipping point so quickly? The answer lies in part by the fact that he made his inventions known to the general public. Ford took one of his models and put it into a race that other players in the industry would see. He took the risk to compete with other automobiles that had been invented, and because of his persistent work and extreme passion, many others watched his vehicle's performance trump the competition.

As an entrepreneur, you have to make the decision at some point to make your idea or product known to the public. Publicity became the acceleration factor for Ford's idea, and brought about resources and opportunities that wouldn't have come to him had he kept it a secret. Strategic networking is a powerful device that entrepreneurs can use to exponentially benefit their idea's evolution until it reaches that tipping point.

Perfection is Useless While Hidden

Although it is not a great idea to publicize an invention that has not yet materialized, it is very healthy to join the ranks of your industry once you have your product stable enough to compete in the market. It doesn't have to be perfect, but it does need to have the capability to join the industry without falling flat. Use publicity as a tool to accelerate, and your product will become very lucrative.

Trust Yourself

When your product gets attention, people in your industry will take a look at two things: the product's actual performance, and your confidence in your own product. It is important that you believe in yourself and the object that you have created. Reflect your passion onto the object publicly, and people will see more than just the performance of your invention. Investors and partners look at more than just what you've created, because they know that improvements will come.

Don't just make your product public, make your passion public. Take the opportunity of attention that you are getting with your invention, and show the world that you created this invention out of hard work and determination, and they will be eager to see more inventions to come.

Chapter Summary:

- **Make your invention public**

- Networking gets your product noticed by your industry
- Networking accelerates your idea to the tipping point
- No idea will make an impact while hidden
- Only expose your invention once it is materialized
- It doesn't have to be perfect, but it must be able to compete in the industry
- Confidence in yourself will make people confident in your ideas
- Inventions are reflections of your passion and confidence
- Publicizing your passion will show your determination in the industry

Lesson #5: Never let go of the Dream

1903-1908

Henry Ford had established Ford Motor Company, and with that he continued his momentum in the industry by working on new models of his horseless carriage. In June of 1903 Ford came out with his Model A, and from there his success boomed. Instead of stopping with his successes from the 999 and the Model A, Henry Ford did something spectacular.

Over the next five years, Ford invented a variety of horseless carriages in different models: model A, B, AC, C, F, K, N, R, and S. He moved forward each and every time, never seeing his dream as completed. Through each of these models, he found something to improve upon, and with each improvement, he brought himself closer to achieving his dream of perfecting the horseless carriage.

It was in 1908, when this dream finally materialized. Ford had invented nearly a dozen models of his horseless carriage, but none of them met his standard of perfection. But in October of 1908, he created the Model T. Immediately after its production, demand for the automobile rapidly accelerated, outperforming all older models.

Sales had increased at such a fast pace that Ford Motor Company could not produce enough to fulfil the demand. The Model T became nearly 50% of the cars riding on American streets. Ford's company rose to the top of the automobile industry, and Ford's hard work had finally paid off. However, Ford did not stop there, because he was an entrepreneur. While one dream had been satisfied, he found the next one to be equally as passionate: he was going to create a way to produce cars quickly and cheaply, so as to meet the astronomical demand that the public had made on his Model T vehicle.

Henry Ford is an idol among entrepreneurs, but why? One of the biggest reasons was his ability to not end his dream because society had deemed it complete. Ford's Model T became one of the most famous automobiles of its time, and society had eaten his invention up to the point of drowning the Ford Motor Company in a long list of orders. The demand for his product would have been the end of the journey for most entrepreneurs, but Ford simply would not have it.

Entrepreneurs are born and bred to continue dreaming and pursuing new problems to solve. Ford never stopped making better cars, and moreover, he adopted a new dream along the way to create what would eventually become the assembly line. Entrepreneurs must always be active, even when it feels like success has already been reached.

It is a rare gift to live an entrepreneurial lifestyle, and it is best for you and the world if you continue using your gifts to impact the world. Ford could have stopped at his Model T, and still would have lived on to live a very wealthy and successful life. However, it was his further accomplishments in the industry, and the multiplication of his already exponential success that brought him worldwide fame.

Never Stop Your Momentum

An entrepreneur should never slow down even if he is at the top of his game, and it seems like nothing can stop him. You must realize as an entrepreneur that momentum will always take you somewhere great. Ford created the quadricycle, then the 999 and ultimately the Model T.

Entrepreneurs are creators of the future, and you have the chance to be one of those creators, but you can't quit because of one success!As an entrepreneur,success should make you fight harder for more. It should be a desperate addiction to seek more success and make a greater impact

Investigate Every Opportunity

One industry is not exclusive of others. Every industry has its link to another. The parts of an automobile each come from a different industry, each with its unique opportunity. Entrepreneurs must be open-minded to the vast range of industries that lay before them as opportunities. Ford's original dream was to create his own horseless carriage, but because of his success other opportunities appeared.

If you feel like your momentum in one dream is slowing or coming to an end, be the intuitive mind that you are and create an escape into a new fast lane. The ultimate mission of an entrepreneur is to be always creating something new for the world to appreciate. So take the opportunities that are given to you, whether they be in plain sight or hidden. It is substantial that you realize that opportunities are everywhere around you!

Chapter Summary:

- **Society influences your dream, but it does not deem it finished**
- **Entrepreneurs continuously dream and solve problems**
- **Momentum is a sign that your dream isn't exhausted**

- Use momentum to your advantage
- Success should make you fight harder, not slow down
- One industry is comprised of a crowd of industries
- Use one dream to find access to other dreams
- Opportunities are always there, whether visible or hidden

Lesson #6: Share the Wealth

January 1914

Model T demand continued to sky rocket, furthering the need for the creation of the assembly line. Ford's goal for the assembly line was to produce a company factory system that would employ thousands of workers to make a cheaper, faster car. Ford worked diligently until he opened his first assembly line factory in 1913.

The factory was named Highland Park Factory, and its integration of Ford's assembly line was a success. Highland Park Factory employed over 13,000 men, a massive number of jobs given to the American public. However, Ford did not stop there.

Ford believed that a loyal, hardworking employee should share in the wealth that they had helped create. Ford instituted an increase in wages to workers in his factories to $5 a day! This was a significant increase from the industry average of $2.34 a day.

Ford treated his workers well, because together, Ford and his employees worked as a system to create the finest automobile on the market. Workers from all over the nation came, and he went to hire on many more thousands. As he opened more factories with the assembly line concept, Ford helped not only the automobile industry, but the lives of tens of thousands of Americans who found a great career out of working with Ford.

As we discussed in the chapter about using people as assets, we touched a little bit on making everything you do as an entrepreneur a win-win for people. We see Ford continuing to pursue this moral commitment to others in every step of his journey to success. All entrepreneurs seek riches and the wealth of a comfortable lifestyle, but the endeavors upon which they take are meant for the world to share.

Share the Knowledge

Another important point to consider while studying the lessons of an entrepreneur is the concept of sharing the knowledge that you have with the world. This means granting people wisdom and opportunities, and sharing in the success that you both may have. When Henry incorporated Ford Motor Company, he gave many opportunities to his friends, colleagues, and family to invest in the company.

Ford never would have achieved this level of success if it were not for the knowledge and insight that was shared by Thomas Edison himself. Be a mentor to those who wish to chase their dreams and create success out of their ideas.

Chapter Summary:

- **Entrepreneurs share their wealth with their system**
- **Selfishness will lead to your system collapsing**
- **Those who benefit you should benefit**
- **The more you benefit employees, the harder they work**
- **Entrepreneurs share their knowledge and wisdom**
- **Entrepreneurs are leaders that strive to better the world**

Lesson #7: Learn how to fail

November 1915

Ford Motor Company was a success, and the profits skyrocketed after Henry launched the Model T car. He built Highland Park to keep up with the intense demand for his vehicle. Ford's life was on the fast lane of business successes and his momentum as a leader in the industry was unstoppable.

He continued making strategic acquisitions for his company, but the automobile industry was about to be severely affected by the upcoming world war. Wanting to find and end to hostilities, Ford planned "Peace Ship" expedition in an effort to advert war. Of course this attempt at stopping the war utterly failed, and he returned to America greatly frustrated.

An important thing to remember about being an entrepreneur is the fact that failure is part of the job. Being an entrepreneur requires taking risks, and not every risk will give you positive returns.

In chapter 4, we took a look at failure as a "testing ground" for entrepreneurs, to separate the winners from the losers. Why would failure be a testing ground in the first place? Failure has universally been recognized as the moment greatest reflection and learning

Entrepreneurs Don't Give Up

The reason people have such a critical view of failure is because they have accepted it as a time to discontinue what it was they are doing. However, for entrepreneurs, they hold a very different definition of failure.

While the world sees failure as an "end game", entrepreneurs simply see it as one more obstacle to overcome. Failure does not have the final say in an entrepreneur's project like most people would assume. Instead, entrepreneurs use failure to guide them towards success. Instead of letting failure defeat them, entrepreneurs take advantage of failure by molding the experience it in a few different ways.The key difference between entrepreneurs and others is that entrepreneurs don't give up on their passions under any circumstances.

The more that you push through the failures in your projects, the more that you will see opportunities begin to arise as if the failure never happened. A change in your perspective about failure will drastically change the way you see your ideas and projects. Failure is not the end, it is simply another obstacle to overcome in the journey towards success.

Every Failure Brings Future Success

If you've ever heard of the saying "everything happens for a reason," then you already have an understanding of this concept of failure. Failure is not a sign of defeat, but even if you let yourself be defeated, you do not walk away empty handed. In fact, you will never walk away empty handed, even if the face of utter defeat. Regardless of what you do as an entrepreneur, and how the result turns out, you will always come out with bits of knowledge that will sharpen your skills later on. Every failure builds the layer of thicker skin. This takes on the meaning "what doesn't kill you, makes you stronger".

Think of failure as learning the "do not's" regarding a project. You soak in the mistake, and how it affects your operations, and then you remember the steps that you must take to not reach that same outcome. Learning opportunities come from everywhere, and some of the most fruitful resources for knowledge come from the failures that you go through.

Chapter Summary:

- **Failure will come to everyone**
- **Failure is not the ultimatum to an entrepreneur**
- **Failure is no different than any other obstacle**

- Entrepreneurs don't give up on their passions
- Every failure prepares you for success
- Failure is one of the best ways to learn
- Entrepreneurs who use failure to their advantage will succeed

Lesson #8: Be Quick or be Dead

March 1919

The Ford Motor Company was the dominant force in the automobile industry. Henry and his wife were living the high life, and the world had become a calming ease. The company was its own machine, with Ford's two great accomplishments running the mighty operations with the nation at its back.

Although things seemed to be going smoothly on the outside, the internal infrastructure began to shake. The Ford Motor Company was not only creating the best automobile in America, it was also creating one of the fastest growing corporations of its time. Investors were stacking up inside of Ford's company, and with every share bought, Ford's power became weaker.

A lawsuit was filed against Ford for attempting to build a new plant for Ford Motor Company. The plaintiffs, who would go one to create the Dodge Motor Company, argued that the funds should rather be distributed to the investors as dividends. Ford believed that the plant was the best decision, and in order to keep control of his company, Ford acted strategically.

Ford made a sudden resignation at the end of the year in 1918, startling investors and the world. His son, Edsel, was placed as the president of the board of directors for the company. Several months later, Ford announces that he was preparing to create another company, one that was his own and not owned by investors. He claimed that the new company would sell a cheaper Model T, sending the stockholders of the Ford Motor Company into a confused petrification.

In expectation for the rival company, the stockholders sold their stock in an attempt to leave the company with the profits they had, while Ford secretly bought the stock. Once almost all of the stock had been sold to Ford, he revealed that his announcement was untrue. Ford's strategic move had won the war against the stockholders, and had finally retaken his thrown as the true owner of the company.

The world of business is full of a mix of personality types. Some corporate leaders create a happy atmosphere for everyone involved, and live on the morally justified business ethics.Unfortunately, another large part of thebusinessmenby people who will do anything to get their hands on what you have created.

Ford experienced this through the force of his stockholders who wanted to see personal gain instead of further expanding the company. Ford had his dream interrupted by the greed of others, and had to think on his feet to regain the control that he needed to make his own decisions.

As an entrepreneur, you are going to interact with many different kinds of people. People are assets, but it all depends on the type of person that you meet. Many people will be excellent members of your team and will help you and your ideas soar into new levels of success, while others will taint what you have made and will betray your trust because of their own personal desires. This is every entrepreneur's nightmare, but it is something that happens quite often in the business world.

How fast can you make decisions? How far out of the box do you think in times of need? These attributes are important when it comes to facing adversities such as the one Ford was dealt. Expanding your mind and looking for ways to out fox the competition is fundamental for entrepreneurs. Whether it be new obstacles to overcome, or relations to balance out with others, the ability to be versatile will be required in almost every situation that an entrepreneur will face.

Insight Creates Opportunities

Entrepreneurs must have the special ability to keep track simultaneously of two different periods of time. While most people handle their present and their

46

future separately, people running companies and inventing products must be able to streamline that process. It takes quick thinking to have the ability to keep track of the present variables in order to plan and execute decisions in the future.

Ford did not execute his plan for taking his company back in one day, nor did he make the plan up on the fly. Ford was a methodical man, and was extremely intelligent with common sense. Ford saw the variables that were presented to him, and he created decisions in the present that would reflect his plans and decisions in the future. With almost flawless effort Ford's planning worked, and he took back his company.

If you can be one step ahead of the competition, than you will succeed in your industry. Inventing is nothing more than improving upon what your competitors had formerly made. If you can master this art, then the world of business will be malleable, and you will see opportunities sprouting in fields.

Be Prepared for Others to Fail

As charming as people may seem, not everyone will have the best intentions, and not everyone will have the strongest heart for what you want to do. You must be considerate to the fact that just like you, not everyone is perfect, and no one ever will be. The emphasis that I have been making on failure should be distributed towards everyone that you make connections with, regardless of how talented they may be.

Increasing your tolerance towards others will make you a more versatile entrepreneur. However, placing too much expectations on people to do too much will only lead to them disappointing you. So be generous to everyone, but do not allow yourself to give too much to those that don't deserve it. Having a quick mind means also have a quick judgment of people. Picking up personality traits easily will allow your decisions with people to be smooth.

Use people as assets, and share with them inspiring knowledge that can help better their lives, but make sure that you be very aware of their intentions. Failure because of objective decisions can be easily fixed, but failure by people can be hard to decipher. Because of this, it is best that we avoid making the wrong mistakes with the wrong people at all costs.

Chapter Summary:

- **There are many types of people in the business world**
- **Entrepreneurs must be versatile socially and intellectually**

- Have a quick mind about your decisions
- Thinking ahead will bring opportunities
- Use the present to plan for the future
- Planning leads to upping the competition
- Don't expect too much of people
- Apply the rules of this book to others too
- Be careful choosing the ones to trust

Lesson #9: Don't get Caught Up!

March 1927

Ford's Model T was his prized possession. It was the product of over 10 years of constant work and experimentation. Model T did not come over night, nor was it the original plan, because it took many improvements to transform itself into a stellar product. Ford's dream was realized through the production of that car, and he felt comfortable with that dream being achieved.

He continued to produce the Model T for almost 15 years, but in 1926, he received information that his stockholders wished to see the Model T discontinued. Edsel and his brother-in-law came to Ford in an attempt to persuade him to make a massive change in the company by transitioning to a new model of car. Ford unimpressed, and despite the slumping sales in the Model T, Ford refused to make the changes.

It was only until a year later when Ford made the decision to stop production of the Model T, and create a new model. The 15 millionth Model T sold was a sentimental celebration of the dream car he had created.

With that, he designed the newest model, the Model A, and set out to prepare the company for its production.

It was not easy for Ford, as he saw his company take a large blow in sales and scale as the entire company transitioned its equipment for the Model A. As painful as the sight was, Ford knew that it was time to move on to another improvement to his dream, and he continued on to produce the Model A for the Ford Motor Company, leaving the Model T behind in his memory.

The life of an entrepreneur can get comfortable once everything begins to go well. The business is booming, the operations are automated, and you get to sit back, relax, and enjoy life. This is the dream lifestyle of an entrepreneur, and it seems to be the end of troubles for most.

However, passionate entrepreneurs should not base their life on one accomplishment. Ford was prepared to let his sales continue to slump, for no good reason other than the fact that it was his best invention so far. He was emotionally tied to his invention, and didn't want to see it go. We tend to hold onto our greatest accomplishments, and we will do anything we can to let that be our legacy. Entrepreneurs keep that great accomplishment because they think that it is as far as they can go.

I'm here to tell you that you shouldn't get caught up in the completion of a single dream. The greatest entrepreneurs accomplished multiple dreams, and changed the world because of it. Allowing yourself to get too comfortable will make you an unproductive business man, and will slow your dreaming. Ford almost let this happen, and he fought tooth and nail with his executives to keep his dream at the front of the company.

Letting go of the greatest accomplishment you have in search of another is one of the hardest decisions an entrepreneur can make, because it is taking your prized possession out of the spotlight, and humbling you back into the same position as you were in before. It is a risk to let go of that dream and reach for another, but as we have already made clear, risks are what makes entrepreneurs great.

Be an Entrepreneur for Others

There are two different types of entrepreneurs in the world. They both solve problems, but one of them affects the world more positively. The first simply solves a problem to further their personal ambition. The second solves problems with other people's needs in mind. This is the type of entrepreneur you should strive to be.

Henry Ford almost got himself caught up in his own mind, too selfish to let go of the inventions he made.

He was not thinking about the people that he had impacted, or the shareholders that he had made wealthy. Instead, he was focused solely on what he wanted. It wasn't until the persuasion of his executive stockholders that he broke this curse. Ford's inventions were made to help the world, and Ford realized that he needed to continue with that motion, even if he didn't necessarily like it.

Don't Let Your Momentum Fall

Idling in between being productive and retiring from entrepreneurship can slow you down, and will dull the skills that you have sharpened through your past experiences. The momentum that you build up as an entrepreneur not only defines your projects, it also defines who you are, and how other people see you and your success. Allowing that to slow can be detrimental to your future. The tension between Ford and his executives reached its highest peak because he stopped dreaming, and instead let his momentum stand on the 15 year production of the Model T. He wouldn't allow his mind to wander further than his creation, and it affected his relationships with the other shareholders.

Don't let this slump in your effort affect your relationship with others. Once you find success, your momentum will immediately begin to decline. It is unnatural for the entrepreneur to stop working towards more improvements, more projects, and more opportunities. Without another problem to solve, the momentum you have built up will start to deteriorate. Because of Ford's hold on the Model T, and his refusal to look for new improvements, the Model T became his most popular invention.

Chapter Summary:

- **Don't base your life on one accomplishment**
- **Letting go is hard, but necessary**
- **Be the entrepreneur that builds their assets for people**
- **Being selfish will cause tension**
- **Slowing your momentum is detrimental to your future**
- **Idle time dulls your skills as an entrepreneur**
- **Entrepreneurs continue to dream by nature**

Lesson #10: It's More than Money

October 1929

The destiny of Ford had been nearly fulfilled. He had accomplished so much, and his fuel as an entrepreneur was close to becoming exhausted. With the Model A bringing modest sales, and his company an experienced dominator in the automobile industry, Ford's momentum naturally began to slow with the changing times.

With his company on autopilot, Ford began to look outside of the scope of his normal industry. Instead of looking for something new to improve inside of his company, or invent another product to sell on the line, Ford looked elsewhere, and for different purposes. Ford was looking for something that was completely separate from his company's operations.

Ford's eyes were set on helping the community in a different way. Thomas Edison had been his original inspiration, and one of his original advocates. An event had been planned to celebrate the 50th anniversary of Edison's creation of the incandescent lamp.

But this was no ordinary ceremony, for Edison had attributed much to Ford's success. In appreciation for both Edison and the American people, Ford had planned a gift to the nation during the ceremony, the Thomas Edison Institute. This institute would showcase many different pieces of history that commemorate America's past. Ford's contribution was appreciated by the nation, and this Institute continues today as the Henry Ford Museum.

No matter how much money you make, or how successful you become, there will always be a higher purpose in this world. Those who are blindly chasing money in the hopes that it will fill the gap might want to take a step back. Entrepreneurship is associated with making large sums of money, but that is not its sole purpose. The purpose of entrepreneurship is to impact the world in a positive way and find happiness.

Think of how little the world would have to offer if entrepreneurs simply took what they gained and kept it for themselves! The richest man on the planet, Bill Gates, donates to several charities, as well as gifting money to several organizations in the hopes that he can better the world for all. It takes a true entrepreneur to share not only his wealth, but his dream of peace and prosperity for all.

Think of an organization or a cause that touches your heart. Keep that with you as you make your journey towards success, and remember that you were put on this

56

Earth for more than just the money you will earn. Find it within you to spread the joy, and better the world as best as you can.

It's Not Always About Money

Many modern day millionaires will rarely talk about the money that they have, or what they spend it on. A lot of them simply see money as a gateway for financial freedom. With this they are given the time and the ability to find themselves, discover new hobbies, and explore the world and everything it has to offer. Money might be the medium through which some of these things happen, but it is not the end goal for their life.

Greed will take away the passion that you have for being an entrepreneur, and it will make it harder for you to enjoy things in life after you have stepped down from the inventing chair. Solving problems will lead you to more success, and will give you more happiness in the end than any amount of money ever could.

Some Dreams Don't Require a Business

While Ford's dreams all involved using the medium of a corporation, not all dreams need one. There are many things that you can achieve in life that are outside money and profits, and they tend to bring more satisfaction as well. There is a lot that the world has to offer for those that are seeking adventure.

Being an entrepreneur outside of business means being genuine, and sharing your knowledge and wealth with others in such a way that can bring your community closer together. Dreams come in many different forms, and a lot of them don't require as much intense work as a business does.

Think of the tallest peak in the world, Mt. Everest. Many people dream of climbing to the top, but it takes more than just the money to reach the summit. It takes a higher sense of personal development to achieve this dream as an entrepreneur. Training, research, planning, teamwork, and other important factors go into this expedition, and no money or success in the world is going to change these obstacles, or lessen its difficulty.

So, as an ending lesson for this book, I'd like to emphasize how much is out there in the world for you to seize. It takes a little bit of digging to find them, but there are plenty of amazing opportunities to seek riches that go far beyond money or fame. Ford found his calling by building the Thomas Edison Institute: what will you build?

Chapter Summary:

- There will always be a higher purpose than money
- Money will not create happiness alone
- Entrepreneurs make happiness to make money
- Being wealthy is about being free to find that higher purpose
- Greed will damper your future
- There are dreams to catch outside of a business

Conclution: The Power is Yours

The Legacy of Henry Ford

In 1879, Henry Ford left his home seeking adventure. Where he would end up, he did not know, but he knew one thing in the back of his mind, and that was his intense desire to become surrounded by machinery. As a child, Ford's passion for machinery was sparked by a gift that he was given, a simple watch. We would take this watch and take it apart and put back together, again and again. From there the desire grew and molded into an unstoppable thirst for something other than the farm work which he was forcing himself into.

With his bare hands he created this enormous drive for machinery into dreams that he made possible through his hard work. He worked countless hours. He tinkered with inventions for days on end, never knowing the true end to his journey. The only thing that he knew at every step of the way was his insatiable desire to build the automobile. Ford would have stopped at nothing to make his dreams come true, and because of his diligence, he created more than an empire. He created a legacy.

Think of all the exits he had, all of the opportunities that presented itself for him to give up and to live a normal life. He had so many options, so many days that he could have sat and procrastinated, saying to himself that he would have created the automobile the next day. No excuses filled his mind, no overpowering opposition confronted his dreams and won. Ford stood on top of his dreams, directed every ounce of his being into completing it, and rode the wave to victory knowing that he gave everything that he had to make it as far as he did.

The legacy of Ford will not easily be forgotten. His dreams as well as his accomplishments will live on for many centuries. Because of his tireless work, and the elements of his determined mind working in his favor, his dreams have revolutionized the modern world. His endeavors massively accelerated the innovation in technology that we have today, and because of Ford's efforts, the evolution of the car skyrocketed into an industry that is still very much alive today. Ford created a legacy out of his dreams.

Create Your Legacy

What is stopping you from creating a legend out of yourself that isn't as good or greater than the mighty Henry Ford? The answer is simple. There is not a single person in this world that can stop you from what you truly want to do but yourself. Are you going to stand up and create your dreams, or are you going to talk yourself out of the journey? There are many paths in life, and entrepreneurship is one of the most dangerous to choose, but it is also one of the most enlightening journeys you will ever take.

Your journey starts here with the lessons in this book, and the ending of your journey is only decided by you. You must decide how far you wish to go, and from where you wish to gain your momentum. There are thousands of industries out in the world, with many more to be discovered by man. There are problems scattering different parts of the world waiting to be solved by the brightest of men. Be like Henry Ford, and take the chance to change the world in a way that will leave your name in the history books forever.

The Final Words

I'd like to take the time to view the ten lessons we discussed throughout this book. Bringing them together, let's take a look at what it means to be a true entrepreneur like Henry Ford, and to create your dreams in the way that entrepreneurs were made to create dreams.

As we learned in lessons one and four, an entrepreneur that wishes to be successful must be able to make a leap of faith towards what they want to do. No matter how much research and planning you do, if you don't take the plunge, you will be left with nothing to show for. An entrepreneur must go beyond the average person's determination, and fulfill their own motivation with a fiery passion that is all their own creation. We must fuel ourselves and fight every day until our dreams are realized.

People are the most valuable assets an entrepreneur has, but they must be trusted, and you must be tolerant and quick-witted in order to achieve the greatest things with the best people you can find. Only then will people become extraordinary cogs to help make your business move. The mission of an entrepreneur causes a lot of stress, and can sometimes get out of hand. Making people your purpose, instead of focusing on your own gain, will motivate you to go beyond your expectations. Use people to your advantage, and they will show you how useful they can be.

But make sure to reward them with the same level of appreciation that they showed you. Rewarding people for their efforts and capabilities is the foundation of being an entrepreneur. It is the job of an entrepreneur to help other people around you, especially the ones that help you create success.

And of course, once that final moment comes when success is within reach, and you achieve the dreams that you have fought so hard for, do not forget about your duties as an entrepreneur. Continue dreaming for the world, and never stop creating products and services that will better those around you. Find a higher purpose than money, and make a lasting impact that the world will remember for decades or even centuries to come. Henry Ford made his mark on the world, what are you going to do to make yours?

BOOKS FROM MICHAEL WINICOTT

Another titles by Michael Winicott you may find interesting:

BILL GATES: BUSINESS LESSONS

BRAIN: EXERCISES TO EMPOWER

BUSINESS PLAN: A practical guide

FACEBOOK MARKETING: Business Lessons from Mark Zuckerberg

HABITS: MICRO CHANGES for MACRO RESULTS

JESUS: LEADERSHIP LESSONS

LEONARDO DA VINCI: CREATIVITY LESSONS

MARTIN LUTHER KING: LIFE LESSONS

OPRAH WINFREY: LIFE LESSONS

STEVE JOBS: BUSINESS LESSONS

WALT DISNEY: CREATIVITY LESSONS

WINSTON CHURCHILL: LEADERSHIP LESSONS

DID YOU ENJOY THIS BOOK?

Thanks for purchasing and reading this book. If you reached this page you had probably enjoyed this book. Would you care to leave a positive review in Amazon?

This is very important for 2 reasons:

a) I need your feedback to improve the quality of my books

b) Other people may read and benefit from this book if you share your thoughts.

 You may leave the review clicking here. Thanks a lot!

Michael Winicott